50 PROPHETIC WRITING PROMPTS

TO JUMPSTART YOUR PROPHETIC WRITING FLOW

THERESA HARVARD JOHNSON

50 Prophetic Writing Prompts
to Jumpstart Your Prophetic Writing Flow

Theresa Harvard Johnson
950 Eagles Landing Parkway, Ste. 302
Stockbridge, GA 30281

"Scripture quotations taken from the New American Standard Bible®(NASB), Copyright © 1960, 1962, 1963, 1968, 1971, 1972, 1973, 1975, 1977, 1995 by The Lockman Foundation Used by permission. www.Lockman.org"

ISBN-13: 978-1720363040
ISBN-10: 1720363048

TABLE OF CONTENTS

WRITERS NEED EXERCISE

Prophetic writing is about hearing God's voice and responding to it in written form. For many prophetic writers, there is an inward command, urgency or knowing that what they hear must be written or recorded. For others, it is a loving, relational opportunity to engage in intimacy with Holy Spirit as they sit in the Lord's presence, seek what is on His heart, talk with Him, hear what he is speaking and respond to what is heard with their pen or keyboard.

I believe there are three schools of thought at work in the prophetic writing realm: (1) there is writing by the urgency or command of Holy Spirit, as previously mentioned, which is commonly associated with the direct release of prophecy; (2) there is writing in the spirit which describes *the immersive spiritual dimension and atmosphere* of God's presence in which prophetic writing takes place; and (3) it can describe the intentional act of sitting, seeking, hearing, conversing and responding to the voice of the Lord in writing. The latter is a supernatural place we can initiate and choose to enter simply to be with God and experience his presence. This is the atmosphere prophetic writers want to create, dwell in and learn to initiate their prophetic writing flow.

When we write by urgency or command, there is no time to create an atmosphere because it is spontaneous, unscripted… and by demand of Holy Spirit. The latter two are both encounters we can participate in creating and nurturing. There are many prophetic writers whose lives are impacted by each area.

For years, I would wake up in the night writing from a strong, prophetic stream with tears pouring from me with this intense, unquenchable urgency and command to release what I received. I did not initiate these prophetic writing experiences, Holy Spirit did. This place of writing in the spirit was like a Jeremiah 20:9 encounter. The prophetic writer who seems to operate like this most of the time may think that writing prompts cannot really help because of "how" Holy Spirit releases them. I get it. This was me for a long time.

As I grew in understanding my prophetic writing gift, I learned that there was more available to me if I would stretch myself beyond "the waiting to hear and write place." My challenge was to remain teachable. Using writing prompts during a workshop one day, I discovered that I could exercise my prophetic writing gift at any time by faith. In other words, I was no longer limiting myself to a sudden move of God to write. This is why I am convinced that any prophetic writer who wants to grow can benefit from this resource, *"50 Prophetic Writing Prompts to Jumpstart Your Prophetic Writing Flow."*

Romans 12:6-8 says, *"Since **we have gifts that differ** according to the grace given to us, each of us is to **EXERCISE THEM** accordingly: **IF PROPHECY, ACCORDING TO PROPORTION OF FAITH;** if service, in his serving; or he who teaches, in his teaching; or he who exhorts, in his exhortation; he who gives, with liberality; he who leads, with diligence; he who shows mercy, with cheerfulness."*

Regardless of where you are in your prophetic writing development, writing prompts can be a catalyst for exercising the prophetic gift with in you. We can WRITE in the SPIRIT according to our proportion of faith. So, I encourage you today to see these writing prompts as exercise. Every writer needs them from time to time – if for no other reason than to relax and enjoy the writing lifestyle.

DEFINING PROPHETIC WRITING FLOW

In the academic writing world, I was introduced to a technique called free writing. According to an article on the MIT Global Studies and Language site, "Freewriting, a writing strategy developed by Peter Elbow in 1973, is similar to brainstorming but is written in sentence and paragraph form without stopping. Thus, it increases the flow of ideas and reduces the chance that you'll accidentally censor a good idea."[1] Free writing isn't about journaling, keeping a diary or writing something spiritually deep. It isn't about spelling, grammar, punctuation or any of the things that might occupy us with formal writing. It is just about an individual's *relationship with writing* and learning to enjoy it without obligation or stress. **Free writing is at the heartbeat of writing prompts.**

The School of the Scribe defines *prophetic writing flow* as a type of *spiritual* free-writing in which the focus is on writing from our renewed man until the writer begins to hear and experience God through writing unhindered. Not only can we sit and receive a direct word from the Lord, but we can also write from our renewed man.

Psalm 45:1 says, *"My heart overflows with a good theme; I address my verses to the King; My tongue is the pen of a ready writer."*

These "prophetic writing prompts" are GOOD THEMES. The Lord loves it when we INTENTIONALLY address our verses to THE KING and use our tongue as THE PEN of the ready writer. In other words, we need to recognize that King David, along with other biblical writers, decided to write in the Spirit from their new man by engaging in everyday conversation and prayer until they hit that stream or prophetic writing flow.

The challenge I am presenting you in this book is simple: Use these writing prompts to get there. My prayer is that the "prophetic free writing" exercises will EVENTUALLY unlock a prophetic writing

---

[1] "The Writing Process." Step 5: Edit | The Writing Process. Accessed May 28, 2018. https://writingprocess.mit.edu/process/step-1-generate-ideas/instructions/freewriting.

flow – one in which you will hit a "prophetic vein of prophecy" and begin to exhort, encourage, edify or otherwise build yourself or the body of believers.

When the flow hits, the Lord's heart will pour like water until that thought, idea, conversation, revelation or expression reaches a conclusion.

YOUR PERSONAL WATER JUG

I spent a substantial amount of time in the country as a child. My father was a simple, country man who bought a trailer on the acres of land he owned. He spent his life raising chickens, breeding hunting dogs, growing fields of crops, fishing and hunting. Everything on the land was dependent on an outside well that had been on the family land for generations.

In the summers, I would walk with him as he placed sprinklers in the fields to water the crops. In winter season, I would watch him insulate the water pipes on the property and leave the house faucets dripping ever-so-slightly to prevent them from freezing. When the weather fell below zero, the insulation would sometimes fail and the water would freeze in the pipes and sometimes burst. One morning, I turned on the faucet to get a drink. The faucet dripped once, sputtered, shuddered loudly and then ran dry.

My father heard the noise and immediately checked the pipes under the kitchen sink. I could see the relief in his expression knowing they didn't burst. He said to me, *"Let the sun rise and warm up the morning. The ice in those pipes will melt."* Back then, we couldn't drive to the corner store to pick up bottled water like we do today in our neighborhood. Instead, the old folk would fill empty, plastic-gallon-sized milk jugs with water and place them in shaded, cool spots for storage. If something happened to the well or if the pipes froze on days like this, they would grab one of those jugs for cooking, drinking or whatever else may have been useful. That morning, my father poured me a glass of water from one of those jugs.

Consider this book as a prophetic writer's personal water jug on the journey to jumpstart his or her prophetic writing life. It may be an old technique, but it is still effective today.

WHY WRITING PROMPTS FOR <u>PROPHETIC</u> WRITERS?

Sometimes, prophetic writers need writing prompts that will not only stimulate writing, but stir their hearts in the Lord. This collection of writing prompts is pulled from scripture and prophetic prayer surrounding The Scribal Anointing®. It is my hope that these exercises will:

1) Stimulate deeper relationship with Christ
2) Encourage meditation of the Holy Scriptures
3) Activate, enhance or increase the writer's prayer life
4) Increase sensitivity to the spirit
5) Broaden the view of characters in the bible and their situations
6) Provoke and activate the holy imagination
7) Stir up The Scribal Anointing® in the prophetic writer
8) Provoke healing or awakening
9) Reveal literary forms found in the Bible to encourage and empower prophetic writers to explore different writing styles
10) Identify their prophetic time clock (see next section), and
11) Increase prophetic writing flow

I am convinced that our Father took great joy in watching the writers and recorders of scripture prophetically tell His stories, writing poetry and songs, and convey His critical messages! While we are not writing scripture, we do have times when we may write on the hearts of men.

CULTIVATING THE PROPHETIC WRITING ENVIRONMENT

As believers, we are responsible for cultivating the spiritual climate around us. No one can do that for us and there is no one way to do it. With Holy Spirit's guidance, each person can create what works for them. Just remember: The writing environment is extremely important to accessing the prophetic writing flow. Do not neglect this area of preparation, especially if breaking through is a priority.

Here are some suggestions on how to cultivate a prophetic writing environment.

1. **Create a special space for writing.** Every writer needs a place to write. In my own life, I sometimes sit in the park, head over to Starbucks, get a study room in the library or even write sitting inside my car when my husband, children, grandkids or their company keep our home too loud or full of foot traffic. I love my family dearly, but sometimes I must find a different space. In my home, I have a room set aside for reading, writing and study. What I love most is that I have a large bay window near me that provides direct access to natural inspiration and tranquility in the early mornings or early afternoon when my home is most quiet. If you do not have a room that can be transformed into a writing space, create a spot that works or find an alternate location. The idea here is to create a point of "seclusion" so you can relax, worship and focus. Also, I suggest keeping your writing desk uncluttered.

    In this space, you should have your writing tools set up: a writing desk, pens, pencils, notebooks, bibles, music player, candles, blanket, essential oil diffusers, etc. If your writing space is mobile, then you might have your favorite notebook, pens, pencils, lap desk, earbuds, ear plugs, mp3 list or laptop computer. I highly recommend engaging in prayer and worship to settle your atmosphere and bring yourself into place of rest and peace in the Father. Sometimes, I leave worship music playing on low or the audio bible playing my favorite chapter on repeat. Leave your electronic devices, if possible, in another room to prevent distraction. You are creating a private space in which to write without distraction in the presence of the Lord.

2. **Set a time to write every single day.** To really break forth in a prophetic writing flow, this must become a priority in your life. This practice will help every writer develop a needed discipline in the writing process called *consistency*.

    Consistency is a power producing agent in our lives. It the CATALYST for:

    - ✓ Maturity
    - ✓ Dependability
    - ✓ Momentum
    - ✓ Framing & Building
    - ✓ Breakthrough
    - ✓ Establishment
    - ✓ Authority
    - ✓ Impact
    - ✓ Development
    - ✓ Success
    - ✓ Elevation
    - ✓ Transformation

    If you want to be skilled or to become an expert or authority on anything then *consistency* is what holds it all together. Period. It is literally the act of practice until a *healthy perfection* is developed. It is the act of disciplining one's self to do what is necessary to achieve a goal or outcome. The key, however, is being consistent in the things that build out your calling not just the things you enjoy doing. **Sometimes, what we enjoy might not be what we need to be doing.** Hello Theresa!

    I know we talk about this a bunch in this group, but it is because it is, perhaps, the SINGLE MOST CRITICAL aspect of igniting your prophetic writing flow.

Repent if this is you. That is the first step. Then, TRAIN yourself to obey the Lord in the area where it is needed.

1 Timothy 4:8 NLT says, *"Physical training is good, but TRAINING FOR GODLINESS is much better, promising benefits in THIS LIFE and in THE LIFE TO COME."*

3. **Put away digital devices.** This will be difficult for some people, but I strongly encourage you to do this for an hour. Otherwise, every little thing will distract you. I always say, if a person can take a two-hour nap, obey none mobile phone rules on a job, or hike through the woods for hours with no phone reception, surely a couple of hours writing is doable. I strongly urge you to make your writing space a "NO DIGITAL DEVICE ZONE" when working on these writing prompts if possible. I've found that there is something about having that pen in hand that activates the writing anointing in us; and pulls the scribe into a "prophetic writing zone."

4. **Practice writing with pen and paper.** I strongly suggest writing the old-fashioned way. I've found that there are less distractions when I apply pen to paper. In addition, the temptation to engage in other activities on the computer is often too great, and I find myself easily surfing the web or checking messages when I should be writing. Overall, writing by hand helps me focus tremendously.

5. **Practice the Lord's presence.** Spend time creating an atmosphere conducive to experiencing the Lord. Afterwards, I sit in his presence, wait to hear the Lord's voice in my heart or simply begin putting pen to paper. These moments are extremely precious. Try not to rush them. Take your time in cultivating this area. As you do, you are also cultivating your prophetic writing flow and the greatest rewards of your process are held in this place. God is waiting to meet every need in your soul in this place. Treasure it.

6. **Choose one writing prompt a day for at least 30 days.** Some writing prompts might take more than a single day to move through. That's okay also. In addition, you can choose random writing prompts. You do not have to go in order.

7. **Dedicate an hour to engage with your writing prompt whenever possible.** More than likely, you will eventually spend more time than this – especially if you hit a flow and begin generating usable ideas. (That will happen from time to time.) Remaining in a posture to receive and release; release and receive can take time. It is also okay to build yourself up to an hour if needed. For example, you could start out at 15-minutes on the first day, 30 minutes the next and so forth.

YOUR PROPHETIC TIME CLOCK

Briefly, I want to expound on point 10 from the previous section on "Why Writing Prompts for Prophetic Writers." This part, as I see it, is critical to cultivating your prophetic writing gift. It is also something I learned years ago as I grew in consistency in obeying my summons as a prophetic writer. So, bear with me.

Many of God's people know what it means when a health professional tells us to "know our bodies" or to "watch what your body is trying to tell us."

The concept is simple: We should be so aware or conscious of our physical bodies that we can recognize even the slightest change when it occurs. Taking on this active role often prevents calamity. It takes training, listening and practice to perfect this. If we learn to do it, we can properly respond to what we hear our physical body is speaking.

If we can understand this concept in terms of physical health, how much more important is it in the Spirit?

Again, here is 1 Timothy 4:8. This passage of scripture is critical to your jumpstart. It says, *"Physical training is good, but TRAINING*

FOR GODLINESS is much better, promising benefits in THIS LIFE and in THE LIFE TO COME."

One of the greatest lessons I have learned in my spiritual maturity is how to TRAIN my "inner-man" – that spiritual part of me that lives in the House of the Lord. As a scribe, this was critically important to me because a certain level of discipline is needed if we want to soar in our metrons.

This truth enabled me to:

1. Sense when God was calling me into intimacy with him

2. Pay attention to fleeting thoughts, book ideas by responding immediately, not later

3. Enter the scribal incubation period (the nudge or press to sit down when Holy Spirit calls and write or develop a project versus doing it when I feel like it)

4. Know what is spiritually urgent for me and what is not

5. Discern the season to release a project and when to let it sit

Every serious scribe must undergo spiritual SENSITIVITY TRAINING in his or her metron. In the workplace, we understand sensitivity training as a program designed to cause people to recognize their own personal, negative behaviors and attitudes that cause them to be insensitive to other people. The training program works toward initiating processes that correct those behaviors. From a spiritual perspective, we are assisting prophetic writers with identifying and adjusting their negative behaviors and attitudes toward Holy Spirit – whether conscious or unconscious.

Once we become sensitive and attentive to Holy Spirit, following his leading becomes as natural to your spiritual walk as breathing.

When we are mature in these areas, we operate on a "prophetic time-clock," as the Lord described it to me years ago, automatically. I define this as an internal, supernatural awareness of God's leading for our spiritual lifestyle. It is his timing and seasons for you to move and act daily.

When I wrote *The Scribal Anointing: Scribes Instructed in the Kingdom of Heaven* over a decade ago, I had an URGENCY to finish that book. It was unrelenting! Holy Spirit would flood my thoughts with revelation about the book, wake me up at night and disturb my normal activities to release chapters and pages in that book. My prophetic time-clock would not shut down! I was like a crazy woman. I know many prophetic writers get this! The alarm would ring and ring incessantly! I could receive absolutely NO PEACE until that book was printed and in my hands. Then, that SUPERNATURAL PRESSURE just went away like it was never there.

God was perfecting my internal prophetic-time clock in that season. He was teaching me how to respond to every single request he released for my attention. Without realizing it, I was ACTIVATED and intentionally training my Spirit until visitations and encounters like that was my NORMAL. If you understand physical exercise, then you know that after a consistent regime the lifestyle change becomes a part of who you are – not just an activity you are completing daily.

When I am washing dishes and he begins speaking, I stop right there and record what I hear or sit in His presence until the visitation is complete. If I have that unction to write, I do whatever is necessary to pull into that moment and surrender to Holy Spirit's ministry in me.

So much happens in those times with the Lord that I cannot accurately translate it, but I will tell you this: **Responding to him ON HIS TIME is way better than creating a TIME for him to meet us.** In the Lord's tremendous humility, he will meet us on our time… but the greater measure is when we can sense Him and follow.

If we IGNORE HIM, HE WILL WITHDRAW!

Thoughts and ideas will be lost. The urgency to go and do will vanish... and the Lord will find a willing vessel to obey Him. People teach that the enemy steals our thoughts. NOT SO! Many times, it is disobedience on our part and failure to act that are the thieves! The thief is reflected in the mirror. We must stop scapegoating warfare and enemy attacks for our delusions about our roles in our own condition. I know this is a hard word, but it is life to someone reading it right now.

My prophetic time-clock is sacred to me. I allow NOTHING OR NO ONE to interrupt it. Period. Sometimes, it lasts for days... as I enter an incubation of writing and can complete an entire book in three to five days under the grace of The Scribal Anointing®. Even more amazing is that I know when that book is to be published and when it is to sit.

To master this in your inner being, all you must do is remain *sensitive* to the leading of Holy Spirit in your prophetic writing area. I often pray, *"Holy Spirit I don't want to miss God when he calls me for intimacy. Alert me, and teach me how to respond."*

Get ready to be inconvenienced! Get ready for the timing to be off when he does! But rest assured that when HE CALLS, he has made provision for the interruption.

> ➤ **WARNING:** Just because you are sensitive to the spirit in other areas, does not mean that sensitivity has transferred into YOUR prophetic writing realm. This is a specialty area and often requires a greater measure of training or, should I say, a different kind of training using different tools – like these writing prompts.

Cultivate the prophetic scribal time clock in you!

Jeremiah 8:7 says, *"Even the stork in the sky knows her appointed seasons, and the dove, the swift and the thrush observe the time of their migration. But my people do not know the requirements of the LORD."*

ENGAGING WITH YOUR WRITING PROMPTS

With general writing prompts, the writer is expected to read the writing assignment and jump directly into free writing. You can do this. However, I long to see the writer connect with Holy Spirit. These writing prompts are designed to engage the writer in a greater spiritual experience – which includes the realm of prophecy and exercising the holy imagination.

Imagination is the human faculty given to us by the Lord that allows us to form creative ideas or concepts. It's the same place people get witty ideas for inventions, designs and so forth. The concept of a *holy* imagination is that place in our new man in which our renewed minds allow us to operate in creativity. Remember, we are made in the image of God who created the universe and provided that long discourse to Job concerning who He is!

I often think about the imagination of small children. They are wired to IMAGINE... and so are we! Children can take a box and make a spaceship or a race car out of it; or an adult can have idea for an amazing bridge design. One of the greatest gifts we have received from God is our imagination! AND, he desires that we use it. I also think of the beauty of visual artists, playwrights, storytellers or chefs.

Luke 6:45a says, *"The good man out of the good [a]treasure of his heart brings forth what is good..."*

For a long time in my faith, I was a shamed of my imagination. It wasn't encouraged in the church of my youth. Knowing the scriptures and following the Law was preeminent. The only pictures I saw in the church was of the Last Supper, the manger scene or an image of Jesus on the wall. There was never any mention of letter writing, novels, poetry, books, etc. outside of the Sunday School lessons, weekly Bible Studies and sermons. The congregation today is so much further advanced than the hardcore, Pentecostal church of my youth.

I thank God daily that I followed the leading of Holy Spirit in my latter years. Be empowered in your Christ-centered imagination!

Ephesians 1:17-18 says, *"...that the God of our Lord Jesus Christ, the Father of glory, **may give you the Spirit of wisdom and of revelation in the knowledge of him, having the eyes of your hearts enlightened,** that **you may know** what is the hope to which he has called you, what are the riches of his glorious inheritance in the saints..."*

I firmly believe that our holy imaginations are generated by the Spirit of wisdom and the revelatory knowledge of God within us after the eyes of our hearts are opened. I also believe that we have the Lord's express permission to represent his heart for us in the earth.

A FEW LITERARY FORMS

I also added a twist to this book. I wanted to talk some about the various literary forms that are found in the scriptures. I want to note, however, that the writers of the Bible never make a claim to writing in these forms or even expressing a level of understanding anything about literary form. But as our knowledge of the literary realm has increased, scholars can now look at the Bible and see so many of the literary techniques that we recognize today in academia.

I thought it might be fun to know that these biblical, prophetic writers of the bible were employing some of these literary forms unaware as they wrote. As a result, *some of the writing* prompts that pull from scriptural exercises will reinforce these truths. In no way is this an exhaustive list. The idea is to simply affirm varying areas of interests that you may have in your calling to write prophetically. I pray that it helps prophetic writers stretch themselves beyond the realm of prophecy, recording dreams and visions and developing bible studies. There's room for fiction writers, mystery writers, poets, spoken word artists, letter writers, script writers, fantasy writers, etc.

I also provide a brief definition of the literary form in the prompt or in the footnotes, and a reference concerning the original source of the material.

Finally, I want to encourage you with this scripture: 1 John 1 says, *"These things we write, so that our joy may be made complete."* Use these writing prompts to write for joy.

50 PROPHETIC WRITING PROMPTS TO JUMPSTART YOUR PROPHETIC WRITING FLOW

1) Write about the most difficult writing struggle you are experiencing right now or have experienced in detail. As the Lord ministers to your spirit write what you sense, feel, see or hear. Where are you in your healing journey? (Writing this way is known as *realism*. It is a literary technique that reaches into ordinary life for its subject matter.[2] The bible is very realistic and includes real life pictures of violence, sex, hardship, war, etc. vs. the false ideology of a sweet and nice book.[3] It captures the reality of life as we know it.)

_____

_____

_____

_____

_____

_____

_____

_____

_____

_____

_____

_____

_____

_____

_____

_____

_____

_____

_____

_____

---

[2] Ryken, L. (2014). A complete handbook of literary forms in the Bible. Wheaton, IL: Crossway, 68-69.
[3] Ibid.

2) Write the negative, ungodly thoughts and beliefs you have or that have been spoken over you concerning your writing. Then, use a marker to blot them out or draw a line through them. They are lies and need to be discarded. In the second part of this writing prompt, write a list positive thoughts and beliefs you have or that have been spoken over you. Use them as declarations.

_____

_____

_____

_____

_____

_____

_____

_____

_____

_____

_____

_____

_____

_____

_____

_____

_____

_____

_____

_____

_____

_____

_____

_____

_____

_____

_____

_____

_____

_____

_____

_____

_____

_____

_____

3) What is the most memorable, encouraging prophetic word you have received from someone. Explain why this word is important to you? How did it reveal the heart of the Lord for you in that season?

_____

_____

_____

_____

_____

_____

_____

_____

_____

_____

_____

_____

_____

_____

_____

_____

_____

_____

_____

_____

_____

_____

_____

_____

_____

_____

_____

_____

_____

_____

_____

_____

_____

4) Psalm 37:4 says, *"Delight yourself in the Lord; and He will give you the desires of your heart."* Make a list of 10 personal things you desire to accomplish in your prophetic writing journey.

_____

_____

_____

_____

_____

_____

_____

_____

_____

_____

_____

_____

_____

_____

_____

_____

_____

_____

_____

_____

_____

_____

_____

_____

_____

_____

_____

_____

_____

_____

_____

_____

_____

_____

_____

_____

_____

_____

_____

5) Paul and Silas lived out an amazing prison *escape story*[4] in Acts 16:16-40. Write your own story about a miraculous escape from a negative situation in your life at the hand of God or re-tell their story with a modern twist. (An **escape story** is a narrative genre in which the central event is an escape from danger or imprisonment.[5])

_____

_____

_____

_____

_____

_____

_____

_____

_____

_____

_____

_____

_____

_____

_____

_____

_____

_____

_____

_____

_____

_____

_____

_____

_____

_____

_____

_____

_____

_____

_____

---

[4] Ibid, 84.
[5] Ibid.

6) Psalm 139:15 says, *"My frame was not hidden from You when I was made in secret and skillfully wrought in the depths of the earth."* Write a letter to a stranger who feels as if their life means nothing. Using this passage, explain that they were chosen and designed by the love of God. (The **good-place motif** paints a picture of a redemptive place that embodies an ideal that the author is affirming.[6])

---

[6] Ibid, 96.

7) 1 John 4:16, *"We have come to know and have believed the love which God has for us. God is love, and the one who abides in love abides in God, and God abides in him."* Describe what it means to abide in God's love in your own life. What does that look like? How is it demonstrated around your friends and enemies? Provide as much detail as possible.

8) Can you remember the first time you heard the Lord's voice? What did he say, what were you doing, how did you feel, how was your life impacted?

_____

_____

_____

_____

_____

_____

_____

_____

_____

_____

_____

_____

_____

_____

_____

_____

_____

_____

_____

_____

_____

_____

_____

_____

_____

_____

_____

_____

_____

_____

_____

_____

_____

_____

_____

9) Exodus 33:14 says, *"And he said, my presence will be with you wherever you go."* Write about a time when you were immersed in the presence of the Lord so strongly that you knew He was truly with you. Where were you? What was happening? Who was with you? What did you experience, etc.?

_____

_____

_____

_____

_____

_____

_____

_____

_____

_____

_____

_____

_____

_____

_____

_____

_____

_____

_____

_____

_____

_____

_____

_____

_____

_____

_____

_____

_____

_____

_____

_____

10) Philippians 3:7-10 says, *"But whatever things were gain to me, those things I have counted as loss for the sake of Christ. 8 More than that, I count all things to be loss [c]in view of the surpassing value of [d]knowing Christ Jesus my Lord, [e]for whom I have suffered the loss of all things, and count them but rubbish so that I may gain Christ, 9 and may be found in Him..."* Write about how this specific truth is being or has been walked out in your daily life with Christ in humility.

_____
_____
_____
_____
_____
_____
_____
_____
_____
_____
_____
_____
_____
_____
_____
_____
_____
_____
_____
_____
_____
_____
_____
_____
_____
_____
_____
_____
_____

11) In Jeremiah 26, we learn that a mob of priests and prophets grabbed the prophet Jeremiah for releasing God's judgment over them. They shouted, *"Kill him!"* Put yourself in Jeremiah's shoes. Using dialogue, describe how Jeremiah might have defended himself against his accusers using dialogue? Be sure to demonstrate his emotions (***Dramatic monologue*** is a literary work in which a speaker addresses an applied but silent audience and in which the details keep the dramatic situation alive in a reader's awareness.[7])

---

[7] Ibid, 67.

12) 1 Kings 3:16-28 is a *conflict story*, a literary form in the Bible in which the narrative plot is focused on a conflict.[8] Solomon ordered two prostitutes to split a baby in half to settle a dispute over who was the child's mother. Become an eyewitness. In your own words, write this story with a 21st century twist.

_____

_____

_____

_____

_____

_____

_____

_____

_____

_____

_____

_____

_____

_____

_____

_____

_____

_____

_____

_____

_____

_____

_____

_____

_____

_____

_____

_____

_____

_____

_____

_____

_____

_____

_____

_____

_____

_____

_____

[8] Ibid, 47-48.

13) Psalm 19 is a unique poem about our relationship to God's creation, nature.[9] Read this passage and rewrite it line-by-line. (***Nature psalms*** praise nature for its beauty, power and provision; uses evocative word pictures that awaken our experiences with nature, and personifies nature to show its relationship to people.[10])

_____

_____

_____

_____

_____

_____

_____

_____

_____

_____

_____

_____

_____

_____

_____

_____

_____

_____

_____

_____

_____

_____

_____

_____

_____

_____

_____

_____

_____

[9] Ibid, 132.
[10] Ibid, 131.

14) In Luke 22:54, Peter ran away when Christ was arrested and denied knowing him. Write honestly about how you have responded to rejection in your own life. Write a Christ-centered vision for forgiving those who have rejected you. (The *reconciliation story* is a core theme in scripture. It is defined as a type of story in which the main characters give up their hostility for forgiveness.[11] All forgiveness stories foreshadow Christ's forgiveness to us.)

_____

_____

_____

_____

_____

_____

_____

_____

_____

_____

_____

_____

_____

_____

_____

_____

_____

_____

_____

_____

_____

_____

_____

_____

_____

_____

[11] Ibid, 171

15) Exodus 14:4 says, *"The Lord will fight for you while you keep silent."* Describe a time in your life in which you experienced extreme difficulty – perhaps in your health, marriage, parental relationships, etc. that was so difficult you were not sure that you would make it. Describe, as simply as you can, how the Lord has carried or is carrying your through this ordeal. (This is called an ***ordeal story***, a difficult or painful situation that tests a person's ability or endurance.[12])

_____

12 Ibid, 135.

16) The story of Joseph is considered a ***point of view story***.[13] Point of view stories are written from the narrator's perspective. Consider Joseph's encounter with Potiphar's wife in Genesis 39. Re-tell Joseph's harrowing encounter with her from the "the wife's" perspective. Expose the evil nature of her character in your response.

_____

_____

_____

_____

_____

_____

_____

_____

_____

_____

_____

_____

_____

_____

_____

_____

_____

_____

_____

_____

_____

_____

_____

_____

_____

_____

_____

_____

_____

_____

_____

_____

[13]Ibid, 135-136.

17) The scriptures are filled with ***praise psalms***, which specifically exalts God.[14] They include a formal call to praise, the praise itself and a note of closure at the end.[15] Read Psalm 138. Write a letter, song or poem to the Lord describing why you praise Him.

_____

_____

_____

_____

_____

_____

_____

_____

_____

_____

_____

_____

_____

_____

_____

_____

_____

_____

_____

_____

_____

_____

_____

_____

_____

_____

_____

_____

_____

_____

_____

_____

_____

[14] Ibid, 155.
[15] Ibid.

18) **Persuasive techniques** (also called the **rhetoric of narrative**) are used throughout the Bible. These are "strategies by which storytellers seek readers to agree with their views of life."[16] Write a letter to a friend or loved one convincing them that the love of Christ is real. Challenge: You cannot use scripture to write your letter.

_____

[16] Ibid, 148-149.

19) There are numerous biblical heroes depicted throughout scripture. Daniel slew Goliath. Rahab protected the spies. Esther saved her people. Sampson was a tragic hero. Describe your **hero story**,[17] a narrative formed around someone whose role is to rescue or save others. You could also be the hero in your story.

[17] Ibid, 100-101.

20) Who does the Lord say that you are to him *personally*?

_____

_____

_____

_____

_____

_____

_____

_____

_____

_____

_____

_____

_____

_____

_____

_____

_____

_____

_____

_____

_____

_____

_____

_____

_____

_____

_____

_____

_____

_____

_____

_____

_____

21) ***Deception stories*** are common throughout scripture. These are generally stories in which one person deceives another. They often include "disguise, intrigue, dramatic irony"[18] One of the most memorable stories in the Bible is the conflict between Esau and Jacob. Write about your favorite deception story in the scriptures. Include details about how the outcome or result of the deception.

_____

_____

_____

_____

_____

_____

_____

_____

_____

_____

_____

_____

_____

_____

_____

_____

_____

_____

_____

_____

_____

_____

_____

_____

_____

_____

_____

_____

_____

_____

_____

[18] Ibid, 55.

22) Proverbs are a "form of **folk literature and folk wisdom.**"[19] In biblical times, proverbial knowledge was coveted.[20] Write ten encouraging proverbs for your family and friends.

---

[19] Ryken, "Proverb," 162-63.
[20] Ibid.

23) Proverbs 17:22 says, *"A joyful heart is good medicine..."* Extremely funny things happen in ministry life whether it is a church outing or a Sunday service. **Humor** is a literary device mentioned and used in scripture.[21] Describe one of the funniest things you have ever experienced or that has happened to you.

_____
_____
_____
_____
_____
_____
_____
_____
_____
_____
_____
_____
_____
_____
_____
_____
_____
_____
_____
_____
_____
_____
_____
_____
_____
_____
_____
_____
_____
_____

---

[21] Humor, 103-104. Varying types of humor are mentioned including situation comedy, satire and sarcasm.

24) Scriptures are filled with intense and powerful *dialogue* or conversations between two or more people.[22] Read Luke 1:11-19. The prophet Zechariah talks with the angel Gabriel about the birth of John the Immerser. Imagine you are Gabriel the archangel. Describe the conversation between Gabriel and God concerning sharing this news with Zechariah. Be as imaginative as possible.

_____

_____

_____

_____

_____

_____

_____

_____

_____

_____

_____

_____

_____

_____

_____

_____

_____

_____

_____

_____

_____

_____

_____

_____

_____

_____

_____

_____

_____

[22] Ibid, 58-60.

25) Write a prayer concerning your desire to grow and develop as a prophetic writer.

_____

_____

_____

_____

_____

_____

_____

_____

_____

_____

_____

_____

_____

_____

_____

_____

_____

_____

_____

_____

_____

_____

_____

_____

_____

_____

_____

_____

_____

_____

_____

_____

_____

_____

26) Describe a moment in your life when you experienced the love of God in a truly, unforgettable way? Did he use someone else to bless your life? What were the circumstances that led to this encounter? Writing about a moment in your life or a snapshot from your is referred to as an *encounter story* or *encounter motif*.[23]

_____

_____

_____

_____

_____

_____

_____

_____

_____

_____

_____

_____

_____

_____

_____

_____

_____

_____

_____

_____

_____

_____

_____

_____

_____

_____

_____

_____

_____

_____

_____

_____

_____

_____

[23] Ibid, 75.

27) Someone you know has been carrying a deep hurt for a very long time. You have been given an opportunity to speak truth concerning forgiveness and healing to that person's soul. Write a compassionate letter to them about the need to let go, and God's ability to heal the broken heart. Your letter must be convincing.

28) Imagine you are standing before the original apostles. Compose a letter that you will later read to them that describes how thankful you are for their obedience to the ministry of the Gospel. Explain how their sacrifices impact your life today.

_____

_____

_____

_____

_____

_____

_____

_____

_____

_____

_____

_____

_____

_____

_____

_____

_____

_____

_____

_____

_____

_____

_____

_____

_____

_____

_____

_____

_____

_____

_____

29) The **crime and punishment story**[24] is a common theme throughout the scripture, whether a person is guilty of an actual crime or simply offending a specific people group. This theme is self-explanatory. In Acts 21:27-36, the apostle Paul is falsely accused and arrested. Take the position of protagonist (Paul representing himself) or antagonist (his accusers), and describe why he should or should not be arrested and charged for the alleged crime.

[24] Ibid, 52.

30) Mark 12:30-31 says, *"And you shall love the Lord your God with all your heart, and with all your soul, and with all your mind, and with all your strength.' The second is this, 'You shall love your neighbor as yourself.' There is no other commandment greater than these."* Describe a time in your life when you sacrificed what was precious to you to help someone else. Provide as much detail as possible surrounding why you took such a giant step of faith.

31) Trace your journey to Christ in bulleted list, reflect on how His love drew you deeper into the Kingdom.

32) The ***divine-human encounter story*** is one of the most repeated forms in the entire Bible. These encounters are "usually face-to-face"[25] with a person and God or Christ. The apostle Stephen had such an encounter. Stephen was stoned to death in Acts 7:55. The scripture says, *"But being full of the Holy Spirit, he gazed intently into heaven and saw the glory of God, and Jesus standing at the right hand of God..."* Perceive this situation from Stephen's perspective. Describe his last moments as he takes his mind off his own murder and sees the risen Christ.

---

[25] Ibid, 62.

33) The ***docudrama,*** a story that imparts information about a movement or people group, is well demonstrated in the New Covenant.[26] In one example, Matthew presents an encounter between Christ, scribes and Pharisees in Matthew 23:1-35. Re-imagine this story as a brief clip in a movie. Become an eyewitness, describe it dramatically for an audience of teenagers.

---

[26] Ibid, 63.

34) Imagine for a moment that Christ is cooking breakfast for you and a few friends (John 21:7-12). This passage is an example of *foreshadowing*,[27] a situation included inside a story that sets up a later event. As vividly as possible, describe how well Christ can cook and what it is like sharing a meal with Him and your friends.

_____

_____

_____

_____

_____

_____

_____

_____

_____

_____

_____

_____

_____

_____

_____

_____

_____

_____

_____

_____

_____

_____

_____

_____

_____

_____

_____

_____

_____

_____

_____

_____

_____

27 Ibid, 93.

35) Ephesians 4:31-32 says, *"Let all bitterness and wrath and anger and clamor and slander be put away from you, along with all malice. Be kind to one another, tender-hearted, forgiving each other, just as God in Christ also has forgiven you."* Use this passage of scripture to write a declaration of kindness and forgiveness for yourself.

36) An enslaved woman was brutally raped in Judges 19:22-30. Read the account of her **horror story**, a story in which the evocation of fear and horror or main ingredients.[28] Consider it from a modern-day perspective and release the Lord's heart on her behalf.[29]

---

[28] Ibid, 103.
[29] Personal note: In this instance, a horror story is one that incites fear due to the nature of what is disclosed. For the prophetic writer, this is NOT referring to genre horror that has no inherent purpose but fear. Rather, it is referring to horrific events that may be true but will lead to a revelatory understanding like the horrors found in scripture.

37) In Acts 9:17, the prophet Ananias was tasked with laying hands on "Saul" after his conversion, releasing the gift of Holy Spirit upon him and restoring his sight. Knowing Saul's past, Ananias was initially afraid of him and hesitant to go help. Write about how he might have talked himself through this fear and gained the courage to do what the Lord required.

38) Genesis 5:23-24 says, *"So all the days of Enoch were three hundred and sixty-five years. Enoch walked with God; and he was not, for God took him."* Write a short, imaginative story about what may have happened to Enoch.[30] This type of writing is known as **fantasy**.[31] In scripture, we see it in references to flying scrolls, angels pouring vials upon the earth, the following of clouds by day and clouds by night, etc.

_____

_____

_____

_____

_____

_____

_____

_____

_____

_____

_____

_____

_____

_____

_____

_____

_____

_____

_____

_____

_____

_____

_____

_____

_____

_____

---

[30] Note: Imagination is a significant part of the creative writing process. Ryken describes it as the image-making and image" perceiving process (107).
[31] Ibid, 89.

39) The ***reform story*** is common throughout scripture. It is described as a story in which "a bad character turns his or her life around and become a changed person."[32] Some examples of reform stories are Saul to Paul, the Prodigal Son, the story of Rahab, the woman at the well, the woman with the alabaster box, David, etc. Describe how the Lord has reformed your life or how the life of someone you love could be reformed when they encounter Christ.

_____

_____

_____

_____

_____

_____

_____

_____

_____

_____

_____

_____

_____

_____

_____

_____

_____

_____

_____

_____

_____

_____

_____

_____

_____

_____

[32] Ibid, 171.

40) Judges 4:4 says, *"Now Deborah, a prophetess, the wife of Lappidoth, was judging Israel at that time."* Deborah is a biblical prophet and the only female judge mentioned in the Bible. Her role was unprecedented for women in her time who were treated no better than dogs and slaves. Stand in the position of Lappidoth, her husband, and describe Deborah's pioneering journey in Judges 4 from his point of view. She was both a pioneer for women and warrior in her leadership role. Her ***conquest story*** is a battle story in which the action focuses on the victory or conquest of one warrior or army over another.[33]

_____

_____

_____

_____

_____

_____

_____

_____

_____

_____

_____

_____

_____

_____

_____

_____

_____

_____

_____

_____

_____

_____

_____

_____

_____

_____

_____

[33] Ibid, 49.

41) Prophesy into your own calling as a prophetic writer.

42) We all know the story of Christ's temptation in Matthew 4:1-11. Write about a time in your life when you were seriously tempted to sin but you overcame. Spend time talking about how you gained victory. (The **temptation story** is throughout Scripture. It is a story built around the temptation of a character.[34])

_____

_____

_____

_____

_____

_____

_____

_____

_____

_____

_____

_____

_____

_____

_____

_____

_____

_____

_____

_____

_____

_____

_____

_____

_____

_____

_____

_____

_____

_____

_____

_____

---

[34] Ibid, 194-195.

43) Casting vision is a dominant theme in the Scriptures. Not only do we see the Father outline his vision for the restoration of humankind, but we also see him impart vision into individual people, family units and nations. Describe the vision the Lord has given you for your life, marriage, family, ministry or business. (This literary form is called *visionary writing*, it is one in which prophecy is released to establish and outline vision.[35])

_____

_____

_____

_____

_____

_____

_____

_____

_____

_____

_____

_____

_____

_____

_____

_____

_____

_____

_____

_____

_____

_____

_____

_____

_____

_____

_____

_____

_____

[35] Ibid, 208-209.

44) Judas betrayed Christ and ultimate committed suicide in Matthew 27:1-10. Write an alternate ending for Judas' story. Describe, as you see it, how Christ might have responded to him had he repented for his actions. (The **betrayal story** is a common literary form in scripture. The main action is the betrayal of trust by nan archetypal traitor.[36])

_____

_____

_____

_____

_____

_____

_____

_____

_____

_____

_____

_____

_____

_____

_____

_____

_____

_____

_____

_____

_____

_____

_____

_____

_____

_____

_____

_____

_____

[36] Ibid, 32.

45) Read Luke 23:32-43. Close your eyes. Imagine the dialogue between the two criminals. Put yourself in the shoes of the repentant thief. Write out what may have been taking place in his heart when asked Christ to "remember him." (The plight of this thief can be viewed as a *rescue story*, one in which the character is saved from a hopeless situation.[37])

_____

_____

_____

_____

_____

_____

_____

_____

_____

_____

_____

_____

_____

_____

_____

_____

_____

_____

_____

_____

_____

_____

_____

_____

_____

_____

_____

_____

_____

_____

_____

[37] Ibid, 173.

46) Make a list of at least 10 personal reasons why you believe that Christ is the son of the Living God. Challenge: You cannot use scripture or look through the Bible.

47) 1 John 1:4, *"These things we write, so that our joy may be made complete."* Write about an event in your life in which you experienced immeasurable joy.

_____

_____

_____

_____

_____

_____

_____

_____

_____

_____

_____

_____

_____

_____

_____

_____

_____

_____

_____

_____

_____

_____

_____

_____

_____

_____

_____

_____

_____

_____

_____

_____

48) Read Revelations 21:1-4. Close your eyes. Imagine you are standing with the hosts of heaven as this prophecy comes to pass. Write about who is with you, what you are seeing and how you are feeling? Describe the level of awe that you see yourself experiencing.

49) 1 Corinthians 14:5 says, *"Now I wish that you all spoke in tongues, but even more that you would prophesy..."* Write out your destiny in Christ as the Lord speaks it to your heart. Challenge: You cannot share a prophecy someone else has given you or quote numerous scriptures. Write what you see, hear, sense and experience in his presence.

50) Write a *creed*, a formal statement of belief or confession of faith over your prophetic writing journey.[38] Paul provides us with a profound example of a creed written about Christ in 1 Timothy 3:16. You may begin your creed with this phrase: My pen was...

_____

_____

_____

_____

_____

_____

_____

_____

_____

_____

_____

_____

_____

_____

_____

_____

_____

_____

_____

_____

_____

_____

_____

_____

_____

_____

_____

_____

_____

_____

[38] Ibid, 51.

WORKS CITED

"The Writing Process." Step 5: Edit | The Writing Process. Accessed May 28, 2018. https://writingprocess.mit.edu/process/step-1-generate-ideas/instructions/freewriting.

Ryken, Leland. *A Complete Handbook of Literary Forms in the Bible*. Wheaton, Illinois: Crossway, 2014.

ABOUT THE AUTHOR

Theresa Harvard Johnson is best known for her revelatory insight, understanding and apostolic teachings concerning the office of the scribe and prophetic writing. She has published, contributed to or co-authored more than 18 books including her signature publication, "The Scribal Anointing: Scribes Instructed in the Kingdom of Heaven." Theresa earned a BA in Mass Communications from Fort Valley State College & University and a Master of Divinity in Biblical Studies from Liberty Theological Seminary. She is currently completing a Master of Arts in Professional Writing.

Available Books:

o *50 Prophetic Writing Prompts to Jumpstart Your Prophetic Writing Flow*
o *Humiliation: A Story of Rape through Art & Poetry*
o *Graphic Design & the Prophetic: Foundations of The Scribal Anointing, Volume 2*
o *Apostolic Mentorship: Critical Tools to Help Creative Artisans Identify their God Ordained Mentor*
o *Identifying & Releasing Chaotic People*
o *Writing & the Prophetic: Foundations of The Scribal Anointing, Volume I*
o *The Scribal Realm of Dreams & Visions*
o *The Scribal Realm Companion (Dream & Impact Journal)*
o *The Scribal Anointing: Scribes Instructed in the Kingdom of Heaven*
o *The Scribal Companion Student Workbook*
o *Scribal Purpose: 10 Reasons Why God Has Called You to Write*
o *Spiritual Critiquing Literary Works*
o *Literary Evangelism Beyond the Open Mic*
o *The Sin of Spiritual Plagiarism: Unauthorized Vessels*
o *40 Signs of a Prophetic Scribe*
o *Signs of a Scribal Prophet*
o *50 Indisputable Biblical Facts About the Ministry of the Prophetic Scribe*

Contact Theresa:
E: theresahj@schoolofthescribe.com
Blog: chamberofthescribe.com
School: schoolofthescribe.com
Bookstore: scribalarsenal.com

By Postal Mail:
Voices of Christ
Apostolic Prophetic School of the Scribe
950 Eagles Landing, Parkway #302
Stockbridge, Georgia 30281

Made in the USA
Coppell, TX
04 December 2019